Purpose: The purpose of this story is to provide
basic reading for children ages 2 and up. Please feel
free to contact me at littleyapperbooks@gmail.com
for comments.

About the author: Jane is an author, designer and
educator. These days, you will find her drawing and
writing children's books. She draws her inspiration
from her students and her daughter, Hailey. Jane
lives in the Big Apple with her husband, daughter
and 4 yorkies.

Author Page: www.amazon.com/author/janethai

for my daughter
Hailey

I belong to:

There is a big apple tree outside my house. In the winter it is covered by white snow.

我 的 房子　外面　有一棵很大的
wǒ de fángzi wàimiàn yǒu yī kē hěn dà de

苹果　树。在　冬天 里, 白雪 覆盖着
píngguǒ shù. zài dōngtiān lǐ, báixuě fùgàizhe

苹果　树。
píngguǒ shù.

冬天
dōngtiān

Little sister and I love to play in the snow below the apple tree.

妹妹 和我 喜欢在 苹果 树
mèimei hé wǒ xǐhuān zài píngguǒ shù

下面 玩雪。
xiàmiàn wán xuě.

During Spring, flowers begin
to bloom on the apple tree.

春天 的 时候，苹果 树开始
chūntiān de shíhòu, píngguǒ shù kāishǐ

开 花。
kāihuā.

春天
chūntiān

Flowers also grow under the big apple tree.

花朵 也 在 大 苹果 树 下 开始
huāduǒ yě zài dà píngguǒ shù xià kāishǐ

生 长。
shēngzhǎng.

During the Summer little apples start to grow.

在 夏天 里, 小　苹果　开始
zài xiàtiān lǐ, xiǎo píngguǒ kāishǐ

　生 长。
shēngzhǎng.

夏天
xiàtiān

We sit under the big apple tree for a picnic.

我们 坐 在大 苹果 树 下面
wǒmen zuò zài dà píngguǒ shù xiàmiàn

野 餐。
yěcān.

The little apples are sour and small. The leaves are big and green.

小　苹果　又　酸　又 小，但叶子
xiǎo píngguǒ yòu suān yòu xiǎo, dàn yèzi

又大又绿。
yòu dà yòu lǜ.

In the Autumn the big apple tree
has big red apples that are
delicious and sweet!

在 秋天里, 大 苹果 树 长 出 很
zài qiūtiān lǐ, dà píngguǒ shù zhǎng chū hěn

美味 和甜蜜的大 红 苹果!
měiwèi hé tiánmì de dà hóng píngguǒ!

苹果

píngguǒ

Little sister and I shake the tree to make the apples drop.

妹妹 和我 摇起树让 苹果 掉
mèimei hé wǒ yáo qǐ shù ràng píngguǒ diào

下 来。
xià lái.

秋天
qiūtiān

We put the them in the basket first and then we take them home to make apple pie.

我们　先把　它们　放在篮子里,
wǒmen xiān bǎ tāmen fàng zài lánzi lǐ,

然后 把 它们 带回 家做 苹果 派。
ránhòu bǎ tāmen dài huí jiā zuò píngguǒ pài.

My mom makes the best apple pie.

我 妈妈 做 的 苹果 派 是 最 好
wǒ māmā zuò de píngguǒ pài shì zuì hào

吃 的。
chī de.

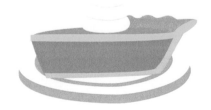

THE
END

Vocabulary Learning

These are some of the new words we can learn from our story. How many can you say in Chinese?

apple 苹果 píngguǒ

tree 树 shù

winter 冬天 dōngtiān

spring 春天 chūntiān

summer 夏天 xiàtiān

Autumn 秋天 qiūtiān

little sister 妹妹 mèimei

mother 妈妈 māmā

big 大 dà

small 小 xiǎo

sweet 甜蜜 tiánmì

sour 酸 suān

delicious 美味 měiwèi/ 好吃 hào chī

green color 绿色 lǜsè

red color 红色 hóngsè

basket 篮子 lánzi

shake 摇 yáo

bring 带 dài

If you have enjoyed this story, please share and leave me a comment at littleyapperbooks@gmail.com. A review on Amazon.com would be appreciated as well. Thank you. 谢谢

Check out other dual language books here:
amazon.com/author/janethai

How Mommy Carries her baby
How the World got its Color from the Sea
12 Months of the Year
I like Pickles

Made in the USA
Middletown, DE
18 April 2017